LOST BOY

Luke Barnes

LOST BOYS

OBERON BOOKS
LONDON

WWW.OBERONBOOKS.COM

First published in 2019 by Oberon Books Ltd
521 Caledonian Road, London N7 9RH
Tel: +44 (0) 20 7607 3637 / Fax: +44 (0) 20 7607 3629
e-mail: info@oberonbooks.com
www.oberonbooks.com

A catalogue record for this book is available from the British Library.

PB ISBN: 9781786828323
E ISBN: 9781786828088

Cover design: October Associates

Printed and bound by 4EDGE Limited, Hockley, Essex, UK.
eBook conversion by Lapiz Digital Services, India.

Visit www.oberonbooks.com to read more about all our books and to buy them. You
will also find features, author interviews and news of any author events, and you can
sign up for e-newsletters and be the first to hear about our new releases.

Printed on FSC accredited paper

10 9 8 7 6 5 4 3 2 1

Recurring Characters

Larder
Wayne
Dave

Brad
Adam
Robbie
Rowan
Alex (F)

James
Dean
Janet
Kirsty

Multi-Rolling Characters

Lois
Jake
Josh
Sarah
Ross
Lauren
Willy
Betty
Jane
The Wizard
Daz
Rex
Jay (F)
Jim
Bing
Roger
Scott
Mick
A dog
Fred
Tina
Tim
Ollie
Johnny
Roger
Dave's Mum

Lost Boys was first performed by the National Youth Theatre at Unity Theatre Liverpool, on 4th September 2019.

Cast

Charlie Knowles
Daryl Rowlands
Jenna Sian O'Hara
Sam Rees-Baylis
Floriana Dezou
Eoin McKenna
Faye Donnellan
Neve Kelman
Kwame Owusu
Alexandre King
Alex Meredith
Tom Isted
Louis Carrington

Creative Team

Writer	Luke Barnes
Director	Zoe Lafferty
Designer	Jasmine Swan
Associate Designer	Sarah Mercade
Composer and Sound Designer	Dom Coyote
Musical Director	
and Associate Sound Designer	Alex Heane
Lighting Designer	Joseph Ed Thomas
Choreographer	Jenna Sian O'Hara
Production Manager	Jack Greenyer
	& Jack Boissieux
	for Infinity Technical

Company Stage Manager	Sam Lewis
Stage Management Team	Katie Browes
	Rica Struckmann
	Sophie Taylor-Hall
Head of Costume	Helena Bonner
Costume Supervisor	Blue Bradfield
Wardrobe Assistant	Ellie Roser
Tour Technician	David Murray
Guitarist	Aidan Maj
Project Coordinator	Hayley Greggs
Fight Director	Kenan Ali
Producer	Jessica Hall
Production Coordinator	Lauren Buckley
Membership and	
Participation Coordinator	Amelia Oakley
Head of Communications	Joe Duggan
Chief Executive	
and Artistic Director	Paul Roseby OBE

Special thanks to: Liam Watson, Lizzie Wilson, Alexander Jones, Evangeline Murphy-King, James Dorman, Kathleen Collins, Lois Pearson, Will Barnett, Ami Tredrea, Eoin McKenna, Aidan Maj and Yiga Cowie for workshopping the play.

LARDER

LARDER OK. Hello. Is any one there?

Hello.

Ok. Right. Great. Right. I'm gonna say some stuff. And… I guess… You can listen. If you want to. I'd appreciate it. And if not… Then… I dunno.

Er… Right where do I start. I am 18 years old. I wouldn't say I'm particularly good-looking. I don't particularly like anything. I don't have many friends. I have a few but not loads. I'm not like an absolute gimp but I'm also like out at the weekend with girls. I have in the past felt isolated and inferior. I am working past that. This telling of these stories is me articulating how I am moving past that. These stories about people in my hometown that I love. I love this place. I love the buildings, and the nature, and the weirdness, and the perfectness, and the people, and the stories and the everything but I still feel… This. OK. Let's start at the start.

This is my town. It's in the North of England and it's about a 40 minute drive away from the city and it's 30 minutes in the train. The houses are new-build; popped up at some point during the latter half of the 20th century. In the middle of the town there is a shopping complex and in the shopping complex are all the high street brands you'll ever need along with a cinema, some chain restaurants and if you turn your back on the concrete and you stand on top of the buildings or on a hill or anywhere high you can see the beauty of the nature that surrounds it. Never-ending fields. Hills. Trees. It's beautiful. Around the town centre there are 20 pubs. One big Wetherspoon's and one night club. There are takeaways and there are taxi ranks. It's not rich but it's not poor. It's a very normal town. It's just that it's new. There is not much history. It's the type of place that if you're not from here you might think is shit but it's not. There is everything here.

9

Everything you need to be happy. And people are happy here… Just because this play is about something very specific let's not forget that people live here and live life and are just great. It's ruled by people like this man walking down the street.

WAYNE What?

LARDER I'm just saying hello.

WAYNE Why?

LARDER Why not?

WAYNE Well why would you?

LARDER Where you going?

WAYNE Out.

LARDER Where to?

WAYNE Who are the fuck are you and why are you talking to me?

LARDER Just showing some people the town. Can I ask you a question?

WAYNE Fuck off.

LARDER He's a lad. You can see it in his fake confidence but tonight we're not just looking at the laddy lads we're looking at everyone else that's bearing the burden of masculinity without succeeding in being masculine. The weirdos, the drop outs, the disenfranchised men stomping around trying to be heard with no one listening. Except Dave. I'm including Dave's story because we have a resonance. Sorry that's wanky. There's something like brings us together. Not like in a romantic way. Ah. It'll make sense later on. When I met him. It changed my life forever.

DAVE

DAVE Thanks for meeting me.

LOIS It's alright.

DAVE I didn't think you'd come.

LOIS Why not?

DAVE I dunno.

LOIS It's a laugh isn't it.

DAVE Yeah I guess so. So you go on Tinder much?

LOIS Oh for fuck's sake.

DAVE What?

LOIS I knew this would happen.

DAVE What would happen?

LOIS I knew that you'd just be shit.

DAVE What?

LOIS I could tell from ya bio you'd have no chat.

DAVE We haven't even had a drink yet.

LOIS I knew I should chat to people first before agreeing dates.

DAVE I was being bold.

LOIS And you've lied about being ripped.

DAVE How can you lie about being ripped you saw my photos?

LOIS I dunno you tell me you're the one lying about it.

DAVE What the fuck is going on?

11

LOIS I'm just telling you.

DAVE I haven't… Why are you doing this?

LOIS I'm just being honest.

DAVE No one's going to like you if you keep going on dates like this.

LOIS Look I'm not a cunt I just know what I'm after and you're not it so I'm just gonna –

DAVE You don't even know me.

LOIS I don't need to. I know what lads like you are like I'm a fucking adult. I know that you're not what I want so I'm going to go and get pissed with my mates.

DAVE What did I do wrong?

LOIS Honestly?

DAVE Yes.

LOIS You're a little boy. You're wearing Topman clothes. You're skinny. You're shit. You're not going to get anywhere with any girls from here unless you get some meat on you, get a decent hair cut and… What's your job again?

DAVE I'm studying hospitality.

LOIS FFS.

DAVE What?

LOIS I thought you'd be rich.

DAVE Why?

LOIS Because of all the nice bars you were in in ya pictures and that.

DAVE It was my birthday pictures. We went to Pizza Express.

LOIS Fucking hell. Why can't there be like for once just one fucking decent lad to ask me out.

DAVE I am a decent lad.

LOIS You're not. I want someone who is good-looking and rich who will one day become my best mate. I'm not being shallow but I just keep meeting people I don't fancy and ones who aren't yano… The One… I deserve the One. This place is shit and I want something to make me feel special.

DAVE You're fucking delusional. I don't want to do this. Fuck off.

LARDER

LARDER When you're dealing with these sorts of things you need to remind yourself you're probably not alone. It's hard not to but you feel like an alien; like you're something off Star Wars that's landed in Ibiza in a human body and you think everyone knows. Rarely are people thinking what you think they are; they have their own shit. It's important to remind yourself of that. Lois is the happiest girl in school.

LOIS

LOIS I'm little and I'm 10 years old and it's Christmas. And I'm wearing Minnie Mouse pyjamas and my hair's in bunches and I'm an only child and Auntie Susan is staying over for Christmas because her husband's gone and I wake up first. I wake up first and it's dark outside and it's cold and I go downstairs. I'm excited. I'm really excited that it's Christmas and Santa's been and at the bottom

of the stairs there are chewed up carrots because Santa's
fed his reindeers and they've been on a big journey and
there's a half-eaten mince pie that I left for Santa last night
and the brandy is gone and underneath the tree is the
biggest present I've ever seen. It's bigger than me and I'm
so excited I can't wait, my skin is itching and sweating
with excitement and I know it's bad I know I shouldn't I
know I should wait for Mum and Dad and Auntie Susan
to come down and see me open it but I can't help myself
I open it up, I rip the wrapper off, and there is the biggest
castle I've ever seen. On the side of the box it's princes
and princesses and rainbows and lions and unicorns and
dragons and the sun is shining and the sky is blue and
the trees are the most green and all I want to do is play
with it. All I want to do is open it up and play with it so I
do. I open the box but the castle and the princes and the
princesses are in a million tiny pieces and I don't know
what to do with them and I can't work out how to put
them together so I look at the instructions but they're in a
language I don't understand so I pick up the little bits and
I play but it doesn't make sense. I sort of put bits together
that don't really go and it's kind of fine but it's not the
castle on the side of the box. When Mum and Dad get
down they don't know the language and Auntie Susan
can't read the instructions either. Dad tries to make it work
for me but it still doesn't but it's OK because one day
either someone will tell me how to do it or it'll just click
and everything will be fine but eventually I lose interest in
the castle and start playing with dolls instead. But it's still
there. Even now. In the attic. I know the castle that no one
could make is there.

And that's how I see life now. I was fed this idea of castles
and princes and unicorns but I can't make it work and
neither can anyone else. I make do with Gremlins or
Trolls sometimes.. I kiss a lot of frogs. It's fine. I know I

could be fine here. But the castle is still in the attic. I can't stop thinking about it.

LARDER

LARDER We're all dealing with things, all of us. Most of us just do what I do and sort of let it fester. My body got tight. It felt tired all the time. It got sick easily. It reacted quickly. And I was trying really hard to be liked. And I wasn't talking. And who I was actually just was neglected. There was a group in my year in school that felt the same but the difference is they did something. They are gimps. There's no doubt about that. They are bad gimps. But they did something to make life easier for other people and I think that like – that's what we're supposed to do. We're supposed to do something.

THE BAND

Three girls and two boys walk on in Adam Ant glam get-up. ADAM, ALEX, ROWAN, ROBBIE and MELANIE.

ADAM Thank you all for coming. I know we're not necessarily mates but I know we've all got a lot in common. I've called you all here to discuss our place in society.

ROBBIE Why are we dressed like gay pop stars?

ADAM I'll get to that.

ALEX And why are we in your garage?

ADAM Will you shut up and let me speak? Right. Fine. We are in drastic need of some self respect.

ALEX Because Danny Corrigan's called you a virgin?

ADAM Yes and the reason he's doing it is because he thinks he can because all his mates are big and hard and loud and horrible. We are all victims of them trying to be laddy. Me; I get bullied for being fat, Robbie because he didn't want to neck ale whilst wearing speedos and getting his balls slapped on the school football tour to Amsterdam, Alex they won't talk to you because you don't want to fuck them and Melanie well… You know.

MELANIE It's because they think I'm weird. You can say it. I'm OK with it.

ADAM And who are you?

ROWAN Rowan

ADAM OK and why are you here?

ROWAN I'm with Melanie and Alex.

ADAM OK. Are you going to play?

ROWAN Depends.

ADAM On what.

ROWAN Whether you're shit or not.

ADAM OK. Right. Well anyway. This is the plan. We're going to reunite the Year 7 Jazz Band and re-brand making music saying 'Fuck You Danny Corrigan'.

ALEX I haven't played since Year 9.

ROBBIE And you still haven't told us why we're dressed like this.

ADAM Look we're dressed like this to defy the cunts that think we should be dressed like we're North Face lids all the time.

ROWAN They'll rip us for this.

ADAM Yes and that's exactly why we should dress like this.

MELANIE So we'd be bullied more?

ADAM No to show we don't care.

ROBBIE So we're dressing like unicorn vomit on pleather?

ADAM Exactly. And we're going to sing songs.

ROWAN What?

ADAM We're going to write songs saying fuck them and we're going to play them. To them. At them.

ALEX They're just going to laugh more

ADAM If we commit they can't. I've already written one.
If you want to just get up and improv underneath go for it.
This is the birth of the small town gods.

He goes to the stage.

ROBBIE
These are the small town gods
Born, helpless, they take it out on people like me, I have felt this
Knowing they have nowhere to go they sow their seeds of happiness in
people like me's self-doubt.

Their idea of man is built through images, subliminal, criminal TV
porn and violence, it's like this, every damn day we're being lead
astray and I hate this.

This is the small town gods' idea, don't be queer, don't be fat, don't
be quiet, don't be this don't be that, be like me, this is all there is
to be and if not you're not like me. You're not good enough for me.

None of us are going to university, I'm just a stupid little fatty living
in a town where the gods don't want me so fuck this I'm doing
this for me and for people like me.

ALL

I'm going to be a new man
I'm going to be a new man
I'm going to be a new man
I'm going to be a new man
I'm going to be a new man
I'm going to be a new man

So that no one ever has to be a motherfucking man.

I'm going to be a new man
I'm going to be a new man
I'm going to be a new man
I'm going to be a new man
I'm going to be a new man
I'm going to be a new man

So that no one ever has to be a motherfucking man.

ADAM That's mine to start us off. What did you think?

ROWAN S'alright

ADAM OK. Can someone else bring a song for next week?

LARDER

Two girls walk past.

LARDER Alright girls.

BETTY Fuck off.

JANE Ah don't be rude.

LARDER Why you being like that?

BETTY I've seen men like him I know what he's doing.

JANE What he's doing?

BETTY He's perving.

LARDER I'm not perving.

BETTY He is perving and if he wasn't on his own he would be saying all sorts.

LARDER I wouldn't.

BETTY You would.

LARDER I wouldn't. *(To JANE.)* Would I?

JANE I don't know.

LARDER I wouldn't.

BETTY You would. Happens all the time. Boys whistling and shouting and all that thinking that we're going to like turn around and get on all fours and ask you to like get ya knobs out or something.

JANE Betty!

BETTY Ano. Ano it's bad but that's what they're like. That's what these are like. They're absolute wronguns.

LARDER I was just saying hi.

BETTY No boy says hi to you without wanting to shag you and we don't want to shag you here. That's the problem. You don't see us as people you see us as fucking… cum buckets. So with that in mind we're gonna say good night. You bad ming.

She goes.

BETTY Come on Jane.

JANE *(Whispers.)* We're going to Spoon's. See you there.

BETTY Jane.

JANE Coming!

LARDER

LARDER I think there's a romance to Wetherspoon's that people don't get. People don't get that getting pissed for cheap is fun. A place full of hopes for a night that's either going to make a life or send someone further into despair. This is the most democratic place in the world. Everyone is equal. Everyone is rich. Everyone can buy a round and everyone can have fun. Inside we see the factions sit in their corners. The old alchies. The families. The groups of lads talking too loudly about nothing and the girls sitting, more refined, with wine in coolers. It's boss.

DAVE

WILLY I'm sorry.

DAVE It's all over my fucking plimsoles.

BELLEND MATE ONE What the fuck you doing?

WILLY I didn't mean to.

BELLEND MATE TWO They're new fucking plimsoles them.

WILLY I said I'm sorry.

BELLEND MATE THREE You'd better be fucking sorry you little sack of shit buy him another pint or I'll twat you round the car park you little prick.

WILLY I'll give you some money.

DAVE Fuck this. Just fuck off.

BELLEND MATE TWO Na take his fucking money.

WILLY What do you want me to do?

BELLEND MATE THREE Give him the money.

WILLY Will you tell your mates to stop shouting at me.

DAVE Listen just fuck off and we don't have to do anything.

BELLEND MATE TWO If he's not going to give it you fucking deck the cunt.

DAVE I can't go because they're all telling me to hit you. Just walk away please.

BELLEND MATE ONE Don't tell him to fucking walk away. He's ruined your plimsoles mate they're 40 quid.

WILLY I don't have 40 quid.

BELLEND MATE THREE Knock him out then.

DAVE Just go.

BELLEND MATE TWO You walk away mate and I will put you through the fucking wall. Hit him.

DAVE pushes him.

WILLY really can't be arsed.

DAVE pushes him again.

WILLY You really don't have to do this.

BELLEND MATE THREE Knock him out you cunt.

DAVE batters him.

LARDER

LARDER Stories are the way we see the world and work out our place in them. We form them; they are life lies. The girls in Wetherspoon's playing footballers wives. The boys playing Conor McGregor. But reality is something else;

the reality is private. Who we really all are; we hide from everyone else.

BRAD

BRAD My friends all tell me how good they are at sex. Night after night we sit around in the Spoon's and talk over pints of flat Carlsberg about how they shag their girlfriends or women they meet on nights out. I'm surprised there are that many women here. I mean to do sex that prolifically you have to go to town and even then I don't know where they shag them. I'd get worried me mum not knowing where I'd been. Jim talks about how he bent Joanne over the rails at the bandstand and Mike tells about him and Sarah in the rose gardens in the park, her on all fours, her jeans by her ankles. Hands in leaves. Him on top of her. None of this sounds like romantic. She can't like that... I mean the pleasure of doing that does not outweigh the shitness of her surroundings like... surely. Like fair enough if you had a house or a car and could go to the country or the city or a hotel or whatever but for us... How can that be romantic? And me... I... I have a girlfriend. I have a girlfriend and her name's Anna and she's lovely and we've been together months now it's... Well it's two things really it's not that I don't want to have sex with her, I do, I really do, I really want to have sex with her more than I want to do most things but not like that... but that's not really the problem. I mean it is. It is a problem. It is a problem that I wouldn't want to coat her face in... You know. Do that to her. I like her. She's from a good family. Her parents both work as doctors and I'm really proud to be her boyfriend it's just that... I can't... I can't get... You know. I'm scared I've watched so much porn that my brain cells needed weird stuff to get going because it's bored of normal sex and I don't think that's true but I know it's true that every

22

time I'm near her I feel nothing there. Nothing. And I don't know what to do. And I'm scared. And everyone says online it's temporary but that doesn't stop me worrying. That doesn't stop me being scared. That doesn't stop me feeling like a freak. Too embarrassed to speak to a doctor – it's a small town; my mate's sister works on the reception and there's a 2/3 chance the doctor would be one of Anna's parents anyway. Too embarrassed to speak to Dad. Too embarrassed to speak to any friends – in a place like this everything gets out. I am less of a man because I can't fuck my girlfriend. And if I don't start being able to she's going to leave me and I get that and if she does everyone will know that's why she left me and I'll never get another girlfriend. And I don't know what to do. I guess it's a matter of waiting until it passes huh. Maybe it won't. Better than everyone knowing. Everyone knowing in a town like this would crush me.

LARDER

LARDER The reason I'm including the next bit is because I saw a show, and I loved it, and when I learnt about the people that made it it made a lot of sense for me. About responsibility and complicity. Not just in ourselves and each other but to a place. We are responsible for how good a place is and how everyone else behaves. If we don't do something everything falls to shit.

THE PLAY

JAMES Didn't recognise you there mate.

DEAN You look the same. Think the last time I saw you you were pissed at your mum's birthday.

JAMES I knew you were gonna say that.

23

DEAN Threw up on the cake.

JAMES I remember yeah and you and my brother videoed it yeah.

DEAN Yeah.

JAMES And you showed everyone.

DEAN Yeah.

JAMES Well nice one for meeting us.

DEAN Your brother made me.

JAMES Well. Yeah. But thanks. Still sound of you.

DEAN Yeah I haven't got a lot of time I've got work so come on spit it out.

JAMES I know this sounds gay but I'm starting a theatre company. And I want you to be the star.

DEAN I'm not being funny mate but like... Why are you doing that James?

JAMES Well basically I was thinking that well basically... London's shit. I want to be a theatre director so I thought why not just direct theatre here. For people like us. Give people something to do that's not just the cinema or getting twatted. Ano this sounds proper wanky like but going uni and living in London and that I know how important it is to have like a... Yano. A space to like reflect on yourself.

DEAN You think theatre is something people want to do?

JAMES Not now no but it could be.

DEAN There isn't even a theatre here.

JAMES Which is fucking stupid. Town of however many thousand people and they can't even be arsed putting any culture in it.

DEAN We've got the cinema.

JAMES Showing what? American wank? It's a fucking insult that they haven't put anything that gives people who live here any dignity.

DEAN So how are you going to do that?

JAMES Well you don't need theatres to do theatre.

DEAN So you want to make theatre and you moved to somewhere where there are no theatres and everyone hates theatre?

JAMES Yes. We're going to make things people would like... actually do. Like legitimately choose to do. Over Netflix or going out or whatever. Like something like genuinely good. Like an actually good thing to do.

DEAN How the fuck you gonna do that? No one wants to go to the theatre it's shite.

JAMES Not yet. They will though when they've come to our stuff.

DEAN Right. So where will be it be?

JAMES Doves Nest. Right in the community centre. Somewhere where everyone in this town can feel at home.

DEAN You don't know this place do ya. They won't come and if they do they'll shout at you for being a bellend.

JAMES It's our job to get their attention.

DEAN I can't do that James. I live here. I can't make a tit of myself and fuck off to London like you can.

JAMES You tell stories in pubs right. Just think of it like that. Just think of it as telling a story in a pub.

DEAN What's the story about?

JAMES It's about men. And about how we don't have to be manly to be happy. But it's like… Good. It's high art for the town.

DEAN Why do we need to talk about being men?

JAMES Because it's important. We're all obsessed with men.

DEAN Are we?

JAMES Yeah. That's why it's important. Because you don't even know. When I look at you that's what I see. You're like… The god of it. You're good-looking. You're funny. And yano… People see you as a fucking winner. You know that don't ya? Everyone at school wanted to be like you. Loud, funny, hard… And I don't think that's a very good way to grow up. I think everyone would be happier if they didn't have to be like anything. And that's what this play's about. And having you in it means young people will actually listen because it's you talking from the perspective of someone who is everything they want to be saying they should worry about being themselves and not like you.

DEAN It's quite heavy that yano James.

JAMES Suicide is the biggest killer of men under 40 yano. Because of this. People feeling like they're not good enough. You could change that. You could get kids knowing that they don't have to be like that.

DEAN Will there be girls there?

JAMES Yes.

DEAN Is it paid?

26

JAMES Yes.

DEAN How much.

JAMES Equity. Two weeks rehearsal full-time.

DEAN What's Equity?

JAMES It's your union.

DEAN How much?

JAMES £442 a week…

DEAN Alright. Fuck it. Sounds good.

JAMES Great. This'll be good man I promise. This is like genuinely important. Shall we celebrate?

DEAN Yeah alright, I'll get you a pint.

LARDER

LARDER It's night out. The moon is full sitting on the black cat black sky next to the stars. It's silhouetting the Vue Cinema like the Hollywood sign in L.A. Behind it you can see the universe reaching out in front of you like a kaleidoscope. I imagine what dreams people have. The ones no one can speak. There must be some mad stuff people think alone in their rooms. Probably some truths as well.

BILLY
I wish I was a little bit taller
I wish I was strong
I wish I had nice hair
I wish I didn't care
I wish I wasn't me
I wish I wasn't me
I wish I wasn't me

I wish I wasn't me
I wish I could be somebody better
I wish.
I wish.
I wish.

LARDER

The next thing I'm going to include is a bit dark but fuck it it's important. The loneliness. The anger. And the inability to deal with anything so it eats you up. Here it is.

SUPERMAN FAN FICTION

JAKE is dressed as Superman. He sits at a desk with a microphone. He speaks into the microphone and records his story.

JAKE Chapter One. The Birth of Superman.

Superman is about to be born into a world that is ending in war, fire, and destruction called Krypton. He's preparing to shoot into the world screaming like all babies do but because he's Superman and because his mum was Superdad and his dad is Superdad he's going to fly out of his mother's vagina like a butterfly out of a cocoon with his fist first. The thing about doctors on Krypton is that they're ready for such occasions. They're ready for all the flying babies and the super strong children that are shot out of vaginas into waiting rooms all across the land so they're here. They have five people whose job it is to stand around the birthing room with nets catching flying babies as they fly out of vaginas.

Today is special. Superdad stands over Supermum as she lays in a Super-Krypton-bed and is about to give birth to Superbaby. Only today there are no baby catchers. There are no doctors and nurses. There is only the crumbling of the world around them flying off to safety in their spaceships. There are bangs in the distance. There are cries and shouts and planes and pods shooting out into the sky. All around there is fire and brimstone and destruction and death and Supermum lies on the Super-bed with her Super-legs open and Superdad crouches and tells her to breathe and as he tells her to breathe she does she breathes deep and feels movement inside her Super-tummy and eventually, eventually it happens and with a scream of joy and pain and fear and life and zest Superbaby flies out of his mother's vagina and Superdad jumps up to catch her just as the walls of the house start to fall. There is no time. An escape pod hovers just outside the window waiting. Superdad grabs Superman and throws him in and as he turns to grab his Superwife one half of the wall falls down and the bed goes with it. Superdad grabs on to one side of the pod as it hovers in the air whilst the building crumbles around him. With the other hand he grabs his wife. She's going to fall to her death. He's weak. He's tired. She's tired. And she slips. And it looks like she's going. It's only fingers and then… Then he musters every ounce of his Super-strength and pulls her up. He grabs her wrist and hauls her into the pods and they fly and just as they reach the end of the atmosphere Krypton explodes in thunder and rage and fury and death and destruction and the Super-family are away. Away into the starry night sky away from the wars of Krypton away from the mutual destruction and towards a quiet life. And that's why they land here. On Earth. In this town. The most normal of normal towns. The most nothing and everything of all places.

The Supers change their names to the Kents and the live on Mornington Close at number 47 and nothing much happens. They just grow older. They remain inconspicuous. She gets a job at the newsagents. He works at the mechanics and they don't seem like they are not from here. They look like us. And everything's fine until Superman, or Clark as he's called now, is 11 and he gets his first pube. As the pubes start bursting through his skin Clark gets stronger and one night as he's looking at pictures on Facebook of the party he doesn't get invited to and the girls that don't pay him any attention he gets angry. And as he gets angry his skin starts to boil like a kettle and as it gets angrier and angrier and angrier he explodes and he's scared. Out of his eyes shoot red beams and the red beams smash open the walls and the walls are exposed and he's scared and he closes his eyes and his dad runs up. It's Superdad but he's not super now he's just Dad and he holds his son in his arms. Superman is too afraid to open his eyes in case red beams shoot out and his dad holds him and holds him until he calms down and as he does he has a million questions. He asks his dad who he is. His dad tells him. He tells him everything and tells him he can't tell anyone and that he has to pretend that he's normal. He has to forget all about this and bury it deep down inside him and pretend that's normal. To control the redness he has to never ever feel anything. That's what Superman grows up to do. To never feel. And eventually. Eventually he thinks he made this up. And he becomes dead inside. And he does. For a while.

End of Chapter One.

THE BAND

ROWAN OK. We know you asked us to all to write songs individually but actually we've been working on a side band for ages and we think this could be a good opportunity so we'd like to share a song we've made.

ADAM OK.

ROWAN They wrote the lyrics. I wrote the music,

ADAM And what do you call yourself?

ROWAN Music and Lyrics.

MELANIE We don't want you to feel threatened or anything. We want you to be allies in this.

ROBBIE OK.

ALEX Yeah. Right. Let's go.

ALL GIRLS
When are these little sisters gonna stand up?
When are these little sisters gonna stand up?
When are these little sisters gonna stand up?
When are these little sisters gonna stand up?

When are these little sisters gonna stand up?
When are these little sisters gonna stand up?
When are these little sisters gonna stand up?
When are these little sisters gonna stand up?

I think of all you girls so much it feels like you live in me
When you gonna set yourselves free?
In my dreams? When they let you be?
What I see coming is a women's party
Top level jobs all filled by me
We are motherfucking better academically
I'm asking you this

When are these little sisters going to stand up?
When are these little sisters going to stand up?
When are these little sisters going to stand up?
When are these little sisters going to stand up?

So here is my challenge to you, go ahead listen
Why do you all insist on putting yourselves AND us in prison?
Why are we sluts for liking sex?
Why do you find the idea of us not being into you so complex?

When are these little sisters going to stand up?
When are these little sisters going to stand up?
When are these little sisters going to stand up?
When are these little sisters going to stand up?

In a perfect vision of my utopian nation
I'll fuck people because I want to and love them because they're worth it.
You'll drop all this bravado bullshit
We'll rise up as humans and we won't give a shit!

When are these little sisters going to stand up?
When are these little sisters going to stand up?
When are these little sisters going to stand up?
When are these little sisters going to stand up?
Stand up
Stand up
Stand up up up up!

ROBBIE That's amazing.

ADAM Yeah. Yeah it is amazing but… Actually don't think that we can sing that.

ROWAN Why?

ALEX This is literally the most like… The most defiance of masculinity and empowering thing like… Ever

ADAM Yeah but it's too specific. It's not including us. It's just like saying women's lives matter and yano... All lives matter. I love it. But it's got to be including all of us. OK?

ALEX Yeah.

ADAM OK. We'll get there. These things take time. Rome wasn't built in a day.

MELANIE Yeah but we don't have the time Rome had.

ADAM It'll be fine.

LARDER

Two lovers come on.

LARDER Oh hello.

SARAH Morning! Why are you up so early?

LARDER Just walking around really. Showing some people around. Where have you been?

SARAH We've been on the hill

LARDER Watching the sunrise?

ROGER Yeah.

LARDER It's beautiful there isn't it. You can see everything.

ROGER It's alright yeah.

LARDER Did you like it?

SARAH I loved it. You can see the sea. It's magic. I fucking love living here. I'm just so fucking happy.

LARDER Was it a special occasion?

SARAH We just became boyfriend and girlfriend.

LARDER Niiiiiiceee.

ROGER Yeah. Thanks.

LARDER Did you have some… Fun. In the sun.

SARAH Yeah. It was my first time. It was beautiful. He's coming round to ours for tea tonight.

LARDER Oh really?

ROGER Yeah.

SARAH Anyway. We're going to be late for school. See you.

LARDER Have a nice day and life together.

SARAH Thank you! See ya!

LARDER Bye. Bye mate.

ROGER Bye.

LARDER

In towns like this it's easy to feel like you're being watched fail – like everyone is always assessing you for not being what they think being a winner is. Like every step you take there's some beady eyes filming ya, or texting about ya, or peeping through the windows… I feel it. But the truth is no one actually cares about you they're too busy caught up in their own lives. Most people are looking at the TV. Dreaming of being a celebrity.

JASON

ALL BOYS
Hello I'm Jason you might know me from TV
I'm an important celebrity.
I have hair on fleek not a little bit bald

I have massive shoulders and I'm very very tall.

I am your god
I am the one for you.
I am Jason
You are in my image.

Hello I've got a white smile. No gaps, whay!
I'm very rich can you tell by my clothes
And the money I have means I'll never get old.

I don't cry unless I have a motive
I'm coming hard like a locomotive
And in order to be normal you need to be me

I am your god
I am the one for you.
I am Jason
You are in my image.

I'm Jason and you are my Argonauts
To me though you are shitty little warts
If you're not like me your life amounts to naught.

I am your god
I am the one for you.
I am Jason
You are in my image.

DAVE

DAVE is a 'lad' now. North Faced-up.

DAVE I'm sorry.

LAURA Just get out.

DAVE I didn't know.

LAURA Fuck off. Get out.

DAVE Why are you doing this?

LAURA I don't want you in my house. I only invited you here to make my ex jealous because he's scared of you. Get out.

DAVE What have I done?

LAURA GET OUT!

He leaves.

The following happens in text messages.

DAVE You've humiliated me.

LAURA I don't care stop texting.

DAVE You've just invited me round and then you've changed your mind at the last minute. Am I that disgusting?

LAURA I didn't want to do anything and then you kept kissing me and you hurt me.

DAVE Girls like that I've seen it loads in porn and pornstars have more sex than you they know more. You're a virgin.

LAURA Stop texting me.

DAVE But I like you.

LAURA I don't care leave me alone. Go back to your shitty life with your shitty mates and never speak to me again. (blocked)

THE PLAY

JAMES Right OK let's go around and say your name and if you were a biscuit what biscuit would you be.

DEAN Why?

JAMES What do you mean why?

DEAN Why don't we just tell each other our names. Why do we have to say we're a biscuit?

JAMES Just trust me OK I'm the director.

DEAN It's just a bit gay innit.

JAMES Don't use gay as an insult Dean we're not savages.

DEAN Alright it's shit.

JAMES Look Dean this is how we do it alright.

DEAN Why?

JAMES Because I'm the director. You're not in the pub now you're in my room and I'm in charge.

DEAN OK.

JAMES James, Digestive.

DEAN Dean, Jaffa Cake.

JANET Nah that's a cake though, he asked for a biscuit.

DAVE Who cares?

KIRSTY I care.

JAMES Look, forget the biscuit. Just say your name and who you are. James. Director.

DEAN Dean. Sex bomb.

JAMES Don't be a prick I'm paying you to be here.

DEAN Dean, actor.

JANET Janet, actress.

KIRSTY Kirsty, actor.

DEAN Hold on.

JAMES What?

DEAN Why is one of them an actor and the other an actress?

KIRSTY I don't think my gender defines me as anything other than a direct equal to all other actors.

JANET I just don't really care.

JAMES Great. OK. Let's leave that there. So we all read the play.

KIRSTY I loved it.

JAMES Brilliant. What you reckon?

KIRSTY I mean I just thought it was so good to read something that's so normal and can fit into any space and is so pertinent to our society and is so accessible for everyone. I mean when I was growing up –

DEAN Where did you grow up?

KIRSTY Just down the road.

DEAN St Radcliffe up on Alt?

KIRSTY Yes but before you say it, yes there's money there but culturally it's quite working class. I mean it's really middle class but my parents were working class so I understand the whole class thing in this like properly. But I know from my experiences, which I don't want to go into because it's a bit traumatic, that toxic masculinity dictates how men behave and as a result how they behave to women and how women sort of become malleable to accommodate that fragile masculinity and that shallow idea of what women think they should be I just thought that was great.

JAMES Brilliant. Janet?

JANET Yeah I mean I just it was quite funny and also quite real and that's how I see things so yeah I thought it was good.

JAMES Cool. Dean?

DEAN I just think everyone's gonna think you're a cunt mate. If you rock up at the Dove's Nest and do this show and make it really try hard and cool everyone's going to think you're a cunt.

JAMES I think we've got to open people's minds to new things.

DEAN Well yeah but you can't just like fucking... You know. Do something mad. It's like the equivalent of opening a fucking... I dunno. Frogs' legs restaurant. It's not gonna go mad busy overnight is it. People aren't just magically going to start liking frogs' legs.

JAMES Yeah but we have to give our audience dignity and do something that is challenging.

DEAN They'll tear this apart.

JAMES They'll see our world in it.

DEAN Yeah but it's not your world is it.

JAMES I grew up here.

DEAN But it's hardly your culture. Look at this. You're coming in with a fucking... I dunno... Fucking avant garde theatre piece written like a kids' story. You're making wanky theatre, for people who think theatre's wanky, in the hope they wont think theatre's wanky anymore.

JAMES I live here. This is my home. I know theatre. We need to respect them and it's you that'll make them like it. That's why I want you in this play because if you buy into it then so will they. And I'm paying you.

DEAN Alright. I guess.

KIRSTY And we're all from the world so they'll see themselves in it.

DEAN You've gotta stop all this yano.

KIRSTY Stop what?

DEAN Pretending you're working class.

KIRSTY My dad was working class so I think I know what working class is.

JAMES Kirsty. You're middle class and that's fine. You're acting. Everyone else in the room has a truthful perspective to inform your work. We're paying you to be here and you being here makes the difference between this being the indulgence of a wanky cunt from London and something that this community deserves. We're doing this so people feel like they don't have to behave like lads they can be who they want. It'll take them five seconds to read a Facebook post. They're going to be listening to you tell this story for longer and they're going to laugh and they're going to feel and they're going to think and everything is going to make sense for them. If we do this play all this will stay with them. If it makes you feel something then that means it'll make the audience feel something and if they feel something then they might think about their own lives and behaviour and it might yano... illicit some change. You doing this is a gesture in itself.

DEAN Why?

JAMES Because you are one of those lads. You're taking a stand against people like you and saying you can be better and that is a life well spent. This is literally the most useful thing you can do without being a teacher or a doctor or an activist or something.

DEAN Alright.

JAMES OK. Well then. Let's start at the top.

THE BAND

ADAM I think it's good we've all come in costume again. Robbie. I love the personalisation.

ROBBIE You told us to.

ROWAN You literally sent us about 10 voice notes saying don't forget to come in costume and make them more unique.

ADAM It's important. This is our war uniform. We're at war against the popular lads.

ALEX This isn't war.

ADAM Kind of is.

ROBBIE It's all bit melodramatic.

ADAM We're doing something. We're standing up to the fucking dickheads. We're anti-vigilantes.

ROWAN Really?

ADAM Yes! We're writing protest songs. Who's going this week?

MELANIE I've got a song.

ADAM Do you wanna do it?

MELANIE Yes. Alright.

The band assemble. MELANIE sings

> *I am so beautiful, to me*
> *I am so beautiful, to me*
> *It's not my fault that they can't see*
> *I am beautiful to me*
>
> *I look in the mirror I see what I see*

Fuck them, this is me
I am what I want to be
This is motherfucking me

I'll wear what I want and I'll do what I want
and I'll be what I want with glee
I'll laugh when I want I'll fart where I want
I'll be what I want to be
Fuck you this is me
Fuck you this is me
Fuck you this is me
Fuck you this is me

ADAM The problem is that it's a bit Liza Minelli Melanie. I mean like it's boss because like the intentions there and that but it's just like… I dunno. If we rock up dressed like this singing like Liza Minelli do you know what they'll call us?

ROWAN Rebels?

ADAM Nah they'll just call us gay.

ROWAN What's wrong with that?

ADAM Nothing. We just want them to listen to us not bully us more. We're not in fucking *Cats*, we're here. In this town. This is real.

MELANIE Fuck this.

She leaves.

ADAM Maybe this was a bad idea.

ALEX Can do. You walking my way?

ROWAN Yeah. See ya later.

They leave.

ROBBIE I quite liked it.

REX & JAY

REX …

JAY I just need you to say it.

REX I can't.

JAY Why not.

REX Because it's fucking stupid.

JAY Why's it stupid?

REX Because it is.

JAY I need you to tell me you love me

REX You know I do.

JAY Yeah but I don't.

REX I don't know what you want me to do. I've said it. It's just that you don't think I mean it.

JAY Then why won't you sing in the choir.

REX Because I don't want to.

JAY It's important to me. My family have done it for years and if you're going to be in my family.

REX So I don't want to. People will think I'm under the thumb.

JAY What?

REX It's a bit fucking gay.

JAY I'm just saying if this is going to end up being more than just a… whatever. Then you're going to have to do it.
If you love me you'd do it.

REX That's blackmail.

JAY It's not. I'm just asking you really simply to love me and not just say it but actually do something.

REX You're trying to control me.

JAY I'm not.

REX You are and I don't like it. I've said I love you.

JAY I just want you to come and sing some songs for one night.

REX I can't be seen to be singing in a choir. I can't be seen to be having you make me make a dick of myself and blackmailing me with love. It's not fair.

JAY I'm just asking you to do one thing.

REX No. This isn't the kind of relationship I can be in. I'm sorry. I want to be like everyone else here. Just quietly happy. Just sort of quietly getting on with it. And this… This is too much. I don't want to feel. I don't want to do things I don't want to. I just want to live.

JAY On a fucking conveyor belt til we get old and die?

REX Yes. Exactly. Safely. Happily. Like everyone else in this town. What's wrong with that?

JAY So what do you want to do?

REX Goodbye.

JAY Rex!

LARDER

Two lads come on leading a dog that's been tortured. (It's played by an actor with a dog head).

LARDER What you lads doing?

MICK Nothing.

LARDER What you doing with that dog?

FRED Nothing.

LARDER Have you been hitting it?

FRED No.

LARDER That's pyschopathic that you know I've never met anyone who's done that before to a dog.

MICK Haven't been hitting the dog.

LARDER What you been doing to it?

MICK Why are you arsed?

LARDER I dunno just looks sad.

FRED None of your business then. See ya later.

LARDER Have you been down there all night?

FRED Yeah.

LARDER Why aren't you like, yano, doing homework or something?

MICK What's the point?

LARDER People do do stuff yano. Loads of people go to university. Or like... live. This isn't like... A bad place. This isn't a place full of poverty yeah you might be bored but like... What you're doing to this dog is weird it's not because this place can't provide for you.

FRED Fuck off.

They leave.

SUPERMAN FAN FICTION

JAKE Chapter Two.

The years pass quickly after Superman's, or as we should call him now he's normal, Clark's first pube popped through. He was, as some people say, unremarkable. He went to school and didn't play any sports, which made him unliked. It was hard not to play sports because he knew that he has the power of superhuman strength and speed and if he did play there's every chance people would a) find out that he wasn't human and b) kill people. Clark feigned a lung problem and watched as women ignored him for guys less handsome, less clever and who aren't superheroes. Clark was happy enough. He takes up the saxophone and learns the intro, but nothing more, to 'Baker Street' to play at parties in the hope that makes the girls like him a bit. At least a bit. But everything changes on a Tuesday evening when he's sitting on his laptop flicking through pictures of the parties he's not invited to whilst drawing pictures of men that can fly and shoot lasers out of their eyes fighting dragons with the head of Mrs Gregory, that she says Hi. Sarah Smith. Now Sarah Smith isn't just pretty she's beautiful and she's perfect and she's amazing and she's the best. Like she's clever and funny and like good to talk to and farts and does everything. She even plays the bass. She's cool. And popular. And she is talking to Clark. She says

'Wuup2?'

Clark is shitting himself. He's got a little bit of poo in his boxers because he doesn't know what to say to a girl like this. Like what do you say to a girl like this? How do you even begin to talk to a girl like this? You can't because if you try and be funny you'll end up saying something like 'I like your smell you smell like my mum' or something and it'll be werid. What do you say to Sarah Smith? Clark is sweating. He says...

'Drawing lol'

Clark is now more sweat and fart than he is Superman.

'What are you drawing?'

Clark tells her it's about Syria but it's like a sort of artistic
interpretation and she laughs but it's not like a hahaha you're
shit laugh it's a sort of 'oh that's cute' laugh and she sits down.
She tells him she's reading this book called The Bell Jar and
it's great and Clark has no idea what the bell jar is I mean
he's clever but he doesn't read novels he reads comic and
he watches films and he likes cool stuff like Warhammer not
stupid stuff like The Bell Jar whatever that is. He lies though,
just to see what she says, he tells her that he loves it and he
thinks the female characters are drawn beautifully and she
agrees. She asks him if he wants to come round tonight to
watch a film and Clark says yes of course he will.

At home Clark is getting ready. He's got his best Fred Perry
shirt on and his mum has bought him new pants. He's told
them it's this girl he likes and they splashed out. Mum's even
bought some perfume and she sprays him with it as he heads
out.

Clark uses lightning speed to get there, obviously he doesn't
want to get nervous. At the door he stops for a second, he's
not sure what to say but he presses anyway. He rings the
doorbell and he hears footsteps, he gets excited, his palms
are sweaty, his knees weak his arms are heavy and she opens
the door and... It's not her. It's all the boys from his year and
they're laughing. Their heads are flapping around like hyenas
and Clark doesn't know what to do. He can feel the rage
building up in him for the first time since he hit puberty. He
can see it all come out and kill everyone. He breathes and he
buries it. And he turns around and he goes home.

In his room he sits on his bed and he buries it deep deep deep down. So deep that no one will ever find it. But it's there. And he knows it can come out. His true self. But it can't. Because if it does his life is over. His dad's life is over. His mum's life is over. So he carries on. He pretends to be like everyone else. He pretends to dress like everyone else. He pretends to talk like everyone else. And he buries his true self that's capable of destroying everyone for the sake of his community. So he sits. And he burns on the inside. And he carries on. But he knows he's different. He knows he's special. And he knows he's worth more than all of these people. But he's never going to show it because that would be suicide.

End of Chapter Two.

THE BAND

ADAM and ROBBIE.

ADAM They fucked up me garage. What the fuck have I done to deserve this?

ROBBIE They're just bellends. Look at this. I mean... They associate music with being gay. That's the type of small town fucking helmet you're dealing with here.

ADAM Me dad called me a meff.

ROBBIE He what?

ADAM He called me a meff. Said that there's been three generations of our family living in this town and I'm the first one that something like this would happen to. He said this wouldn't happen if you weren't such a meff and I was like I'm not a meff and he was like you are look people don't do this to you if ya not a meff.

ROBBIE But you're not a meff.

ADAM I know I'm not a meff but he thinks I am. And obviously everyone thinks I am. And obviously my fucking ancestors are watching over me thinking I'm a meff. So maybe I am a meff.

ROBBIE Who did this?

ADAM It was probably Danny Corrigan and that lot and that wasn't it.

ROBBIE Why do you think that?

ADAM I told him that I was in a band.

ROBBIE You told him you were in a band and he messed up ya garage?

ADAM Yeah.

ROBBIE But why would he do that?

ADAM I didn't just tell him I was in a band did I?

ROBBIE What did you say?

ADAM I said, listen Danny, I'm not just a virgin I'm in a band and I'm gonna get more pussy than you ever will you ginger prick.

ROBBIE Oh right.

ADAM Ano.

ROBBIE Absolute helmets

ROWAN, ALEX and MELANIE enter.

ROWAN What happened?

ADAM Got trashed didn't we. They found out about the band and smashed up my dad's garage. Dad called me a meff and said my ancestors would be ashamed of me.

ROWAN Fuck.

ADAM They do shit like this all the time and we're doing nothing. I want to do something. We can't stop them doing this. We can stand up to them. We can't fight them but we can stand up to them. I know you think it's shit but that's why this band can do something. We can't fight but we can fucking… sing. That sounds a bit fucking *Glee* doesn't it?

ROWAN No. It's important. This is why we're doing this isn't it? I've done a song.

ADAM and ROWAN go to the instruments.

ROWAN Come on.

They kick into a rage song.

ROWAN

Break down the cunts
Fuck them with their fury.
They don't know what it is to be real
Small town gods of violence
Soul of Ian Beale.

Zombies peaking through armour
Of skin and bones and meat
Not understanding humans
They shit on everyone they meet.

(Instrumental pre-chorus)

Fuck The Small Town Violent Gods
Fuck Their Tiny Dicks
Fuck Their Hatred of Normality
Fuck The Fucking Pricks

They haunt the clubs
They haunt the bars
They haunt the school
They haunt the Spar
They haunt the village
They haunt the town
They haunt fucking everything
Burn them down

So warped they have to fight
So thick they cannot talk
So ill-read they have no sight
Stick a fork in me I'm done.

(Instrumental pre-chorus)

Fuck The Small Town Violent Gods
Fuck Their Tiny Dicks
Fuck Their Hatred of Normality
Fuck The Fucking Pricks

> *Fuck The Small Town Violent Gods*
> *Fuck Their Tiny Dicks*
> *Fuck Their Hatred of Normality*
> *Fuck The Fucking Pricks*

ADAM That's boss could we end on...

> *Fuck You*
> *Fuck You*
> *Fuck You*
> *Fuck You*
> *Fuck You*
> *Fuck You*
> *Fuck You*

ROWAN What do you reckon?

ALEX I like the gesture. But if we do songs like that all they'll see is the hate. We've got to be more nuanced.

MELANIE That's basically my song.

ADAM I think there's probably a sweet spot somewhere.

MELANIE Fine.

ADAM Yes. I like that you used a line from mine by the way.

ROWAN What one?

ADAM Small town gods.

MELANIE That's boss. That's what we should call ourselves.

ROBBIE We're kind of saying to fuck ourselves then aren't we. They're the gods we're just... I dunno. Fucking camels. Or something.

ADAM How about this?

He scrawls NEW TOWN HUMANS.

ADAM Gods feed off Humans faith. If humans stop worshipping them gods disappear. That's what we're doing. We're killing gods. And humans are weird. And individual. And revolutionary. That's what we are. NEW TOWN HUMANS.

ROWAN I love it.

DAISY

DAISY It's night. Outside there's rain just like pattering on the window. I've got uni tomorrow and I'm knackered because I can't sleep because Henry's depressed. He's good. He tells me everything about how he feels and I'm there for him. I am. I really am. I actually am there for him like 100%, like tonight he didn't want to go home because his wallpaper is quite triggering so I said he could stay in my bed but Mum won't let us sleep together so I'm on the floor in the corridor and that's fine. I don't mind that because that's what love is isn't it. Love is sleeping outside in the corridor by the toilet because ya boyfriend is sad. I know that love is like sacrifice. I know we have to give up things for other people and that's just fine but like… I can't help but think… Like. Lying here. On this rug. Like a dog. I'm thinking to myself like… I'm fucking up uni. Because… Well… Because lots of reasons. I have a depressed boyfriend. Which is fine. As I say that's what love is – sacrifice and I don't mind that but like… I look at my mum. And my mum has been married to my dad for 30 years. My dad's a doctor and my mum's a teacher and she worked while he trained in a different field and wrote a book and… and I wonder whether mum wanted to write her book. Or retrain. And I look at Henry and Henry is depressed. And it's not my fault he's depressed. But… I'm going to become my mum and I don't know whether I like that or not. I mean… I want to do things, be things, but love expects something different. Henry expects something different. I don't want to spend my whole life carrying someone else's success. But maybe that's what love is. Whilst men go and study, earn money, play golf, sleep around. That's what my friends' mums do, they hold everything together. I lie down on my rug, outside the toilet, and I close my eyes. I think of what to make Henry for breakfast. I think of what I can say to bunk off uni tomorrow to play computer games with him. I sleep.

DAVE

DAVE is talking to a room full of internet avatars.

DAVE Thank you for talking to me. I know you must be really busy but I just wanted to say thank you for making it, I reckon you've helped more men than you know.

WIZARD It's OK.

DAVE Feeling a bit nervous.

ANXIETY CAT How nervous?

DAVE Well like – I dunno it's weird. Coming into a chat room full of men to get advice.

WILLY WONKA Oh you think you're too big for this do you?

DAVE No.

BATMAN WHY DON'T YOU DIE!

DAVE I don't want to die.

ANXIETY Cat DIE!

DAVE No. Right. Well – shall I just tell you what's up?

WIZARD Before you do I just want to tell you there are millions of men who have been right where you are now and have passed through here and gone on to be happy. You're safe. It's normal. You're good.

DAVE Thanks.

A FROG There are a lot of weird people in here but they're just bitter and twisted and you've got to work past them.

DAVE OK. Well listen. Basically what's happened is I've battered someone so everyone's scared of me and I had sex with this girl and everyone thought I sexually assaulted her and basically everyone hates me and I'm just doing what I'm supposed to be doing. Like... Men fight back. Men have proper sex like in porn. I'm just doing me. And it's like a small town and people don't leave it because like why would they so basically I'm fucked. If I want to live here I have to sort something out. I have to find a way to live here.

DARTH VADER You're not the first to ask these questions.

DAVE Then what are the answers?

WIZARD It's in saying fuck it. You don't actually need women. You don't actually need friends. You're not a criminal. Women only have men in their lives because they are either bored, poor, or have no self-esteem. She probably thought she was being a slag and needed to divert it. Don't worry about it. Go to the gym. Focus on work. And see women for what they are. Cum buckets.

WEASEL123 Yeah. Cum Buckets. And divorces. And taking the kids. And taking your happiness. And making you fat. And letting life pass you by as they rob and rape you.

DEREKJACKSON1964 I had a wife once. I loved her. Love is greater than all of this –

*Derek has been kicked out of the conversation

WIZARD He's a regular. Apologies. You don't need that.

TRUMP #1 That's the truth of it. You can't let women or anything get in the way of making yourself awesome. They are cum bucket fuck slags and they are there for fucking.

TRUMP #2 They'll fuck you and exploit you and they'll make you feel like you need them and you'll hand over everything even your life and then one day one day you'll realise you've spent 30 years working to pay for the house of someone you hate who has taken your youth.

TRUMP #3 Your happiness

TRUMP #4 Your curiosity

TRUMP #1 Your zest

ALL TRUMPS Your everything. **TRUMP #1** We're not saying give up on women.

TRUMP #4 We're just saying see through it.

TRUMP #3 You don't need them.

TRUMP #2 If you meet your best friend then fine.

TRUMP #1 But until then.

TRUMP #4 Fuck them.

TRUMP #3 Jizz on them.

TRUMP #2 Degrade them.

TRUMP #1 Treat them for what they are

ALL TRUMPS Fuck sacks. Because that's all you need them for.

TRUMP #2 Hope that helps. Now go and live.

BING

I look in the mirror every day
Checking my hairline as I watch it go away.
I'm getting fatter and older
I'm losing myself.
I'm growing colder and colder
I need some help.

Time doesn't discriminate between the good and the bad and it takes
and it takes and we stop loving ourselves
And it rides and it drags and it hurts and it depletes our reason
And if there's a reason it's time to grow up
I'm not ready for it

I'm not ready for it ready for it ready for it
This is the one thing in life I can't control
I am getting older
I am not good enough.

My friends will rip the fuck out of me
I'm a fat balding no mark in a small town that's shitty.

If's there's a reason I can't be perfect when everyone else is then I'm
ready to die

I'm ready to die

Being normal's not being perfect and not being perfect isn't enough to
be alive.

I'm ready to die.

I'm ready to die.

LARDER

DAZ Why are you here you're too old to be here.

LARDER I'm just watching the play. Are you watching the play?

DAZ Yeah.

LARDER Are you excited?

DAZ Plays are shite mate. Saw one in school and it was crap.

LARDER What one?

DAZ Can't remember it was so crap.

LARDER This one might be good.

DAZ Doubt it. Only here because Mum made me.

LARDER Look here they come.

DAZ This better be good.

THE PLAY

The players come on stage.

THE STORYTELLER Once upon time there was a magical land just outside of the kingdom called Granfton. In it were all the workers that worked on the king's land and they were happy. They spent their days riding wagons into the town where they performed jobs for the king, such as gardening or changing his valuable rocks into things the king could sell. In return the king gave them enough money to live off for the following week. When the money was up they got their next week's wages. This was very clever by the king, as it meant they always had to work and they couldn't ask for more money because if they did there was always someone else who would replace them. In the middle of all this was two Tingos (as they were called there) that live in the magical land. They were Pongo –

Enter PONGO, he is very handsome

– and He-He.

Enter HE-HE, she is very beautiful.

THE STORYTELLER The rule in Granfton was that all Tingos had to conform to their gender. Boy Tingos had to be loud, funny, strong, and handsome. Girl Tingos, beautiful, quiet, obedient, and non-confrontational. Pongo – why don't you tell them about yourself.

PONGO I am the greatest of all the Tingos. I am the biggest. I am the strongest. I am the fastest. I am the sexiest. I am the funniest. I am everything. Do you want to hear a joke?

AUDIENCE Yes

PONGO What kind of a bee gives milk? A Boobie! Hahahahahahahahahaha.

THE STORYTELLER Everyone loved Pongo, he was the most befriended and most fancied by the Tingos in Granfton. And He-He was exactly the same as a girl.

HE-HE I am the greatest women. I am the sexiest. The thinnest. The most beautiful. The most charming. The quietest at parties and the freakiest in bed. Hello.

THE STORYTELLER One day they found themselves in the middle of a weekend. And in the weekend they found themselves on a dancefloor listening to some of the world's finest Granfton tunes.

Cue Granfton Music.

THE STORYTELLER This was the start of the love story.

They dance. It's fun. They fall in love. Just before they kiss…

THE STORYTELLER BUT we don't want to see that now do we? After this night they spend lots of nights doing things like –

PONGO Going out.

HE-HE Staying in.

PONGO She's He-He.

HE-HE He's Pongo.

THE STORYTELLER What do you guys have in common?

PONGO We're exactly the same.

HE-HE Yeah

PONGO We're soulmates.

THE STORYTELLERS What do you talk about?

PONGO Not much.

THE STORYTELLER OK. Do you talk about your feelings?

HE-HE No.

THE STORYTELLER Why?

PONGO Because we're happy.

HE-HE Yeah.

THE STORYTELLER Pongo and He-He get married. This is a brief exerpt from the wedding.

Music plays.

PONGO and HE-HE in wedding attire. They dance.

THE STORYTELLER And, as is Granfton law, the king turns up to make them swear to love each other forever or they'll face his wrath.

The KING enters (It's the Storyteller).

THE KING Do you two swear to love each other forever and if not face the punishment of my choosing?

PONGO I do.

THE KING And do you?

HE-HE I do.

THE KING Then it's time for the customary King's Dance.

Music plays.

The KING dances.

THE STORYTELLER But then things get dark. As time goes on this happens.

PONGO We have nothing to speak about

HE-HE I'm ageing

PONGO She's ageing.

HE-HE He's ageing.

PONGO I'm ageing.

HE-HE As I get older I'm getting more scared and he just won't open up and he won't stop joking and he doesn't love me he just loved that I was good-looking and people liked me.

PONGO Fuck.

HE-HE We aren't actually friends.

PONGO We don't know each other.

HE-HE He was the best man in Granfton.

PONGO She was the best girl in Granfton.

61

HE-HE Then why isn't it perfect?

PONGO Why didn't it all just work out?

HE-HE I think –

PONGO I think –

BOTH It's time for a divorce!

The KING appears.

THE KING Now you know that a divorce means that I get to chose what the punishment is?

BOTH Yes.

THE KING Before I decide. What was the problem?

PONGO She was the best girl in town but as a person she was vacuous and now she's ageing and there's nothing in it for me.

HE-HE He was the best-looking and the loudest and the funniest and the most Graftonist but as we've got older he's emotionally unavailable and he loved what I represented and not me as a person.

THE KING So each of you represented what you thought was the perfect role models for your gender but both were vacuous?

BOTH Yes.

THE KING And now you're raging because there is nothing keeping this relationship together?

BOTH Yes

THE KING In that case I'll sanction the divorce and start a new law. From now on there are no ways to behave for men or women. Boys and girls must dress how they like and be interested in what they like. They must be defined by their interests and not by their ability to conform to what's expected of them as a man or a woman.

BOTH OK!

THE STORYTELLER The next day in the school was magic. Boys came in dresses. Girls came in soldiers' uniforms. And they played and talked together. And from that day on no one would marry because they thought they should just marry the opposite sex that behaves the way the opposite sex does. They married WHOEVER they liked because they loved them. And everyone lived happily ever after.

THE END.

LARDER What do you think?

DAZ Bit shit wasn't it.

LARDER Yeah?

DAZ Well. I dunno. Made me think about my brother though. He looks so sad.

LARDER Did it make you think about you?

DAZ No, fuck off.

LARDER It made me think about me. I think about my mum. I think about how lonely I am. I think about pandering to boys. I think about impressing girls who will never like me because I'm not myself. That's how I started to notice how sad I was. How I needed to do something about it. I think we're told to ignore feelings. Then something cracks them open. That's what I got from this play – even if it is wanky.

SUPERMAN FAN FICTION

JAKE Chapter Three – When Superman First Heard A Song
Properly or, The End of The World.

Superman is now 18 and he's not been distracted by girls
or done anything silly, he's dressed normally, not how
he'd like, and he edited the school paper and he read and
he did homework and he worked out and actually he is
starting to think that perhaps he is quite good-looking
even if no one else notices it and that's fine. But really
what's really going on in his head is that he's just burying
down his desires to be like everyone else. He's kind of not
really thinking much about love, of sex, or heartbreak,
of friends, of memories, or lifelong bonds, or playing
football, not that he could because then, obviously,
everyone would know he's a superhero, or bike riding
or anything like that. He has locked himself away and he
has worked and he's happy. For the most part. He knows
that having friends is impossible for him and he knows
that falling in love is impossible for him. Not only because
if he falls in love and his heart is broken there is every
chance he could explode and kill them... He still has no
idea what might happen during sex. He has shut himself
off and decided to concentrate on work. And that's fine.

Today is prom day. It's the last day of school and he
is really happy because soon; soon he can be the man
that he truly is and spend all his time, alone in his room
writing articles, or blogs, or for internet websites about
the world and be a journalist forever. After today he
can start the life he wanted. After today he can become
the best version of himself he can be from the safety of
his own home. And standing here, in the light, and the
sound, underneath the glitter balls and next to the sausage
rolls and drinks and fun, with the smell of pheromones
in the air, Superman feels very alone. On stage some

64

students are singing. And something about their singing stirs something deep in him and for some reason he can't control himself and as he can't control himself he falls and as he falls he brings down the table with him and he closes his eyes so the rays don't come out and he won't open them. And he can't… And he can't keep it in… He can't… He can't carry on… He can't… He… And then… And then… And then there is light and there is fire and there is everything and he can see nothing and all he can hear is the screaming and the burning and collapsing of everything; the school is burning and all he can feel is absolute catharsis. The only sound he can make sounds like an orgasm and all around him this town is burning. It's burning everything. Everyone is dying and he's screaming and screaming and screaming and he feels amazing. This is him. This is the real him and everything he has been holding in for years and suddenly utterly he is him. He is the most him he'll ever be and the fire stops. He drops his shoulders. He is free. And he opens his eyes and all he can see is devastation. Charred bodies. Sarah screaming. The bodies disintegrating. Everything is in chaos and he is at peace. And he flies off. Somewhere where he can be him, and he doesn't have to be fucking normal to be accepted because normal is not good enough anyway. There are normal failures and a normal successes and both are shite and neither are fucking Superman. Superman has thrown off the shackles of normality in fire and fury and is free and now flying away. Wherever he goes he will be special because he is him. Superman lives. And this town is dead.

End of Chapter Three.

DAVE

DAVE is hench now.

LOIS Hi.

DAVE Do I know you?

LOIS We went on a date earlier in the year.

DAVE That girl from –

LOIS Yeah. Wow you look good.

DAVE I've been working out.

LOIS You sorted your job out yet?

DAVE Yeah.

LOIS What you doing?

DAVE I'm training to be an accountant.

LOIS That sounds boring.

DAVE Well it pays a shit ton of money so I don't give a fuck.

LOIS How much.

DAVE More than you earn.

LOIS Are you like really insecure?

DAVE No. I just don't like talking to women.

LOIS Why?

DAVE Because you've got an agenda.

LOIS What's that?

DAVE Money, self-esteem, status… The only reason you want men is to make yourself feel better about yourself.

LOIS Or just for sex.

DAVE Do you see how shallow this is?

LOIS You're not going to find anyone as attractive as me offer you sex in a gym.

DAVE You're just a little slag why would I want to?

LOIS Women can have sex drives too you know. I can fuck just like you.

DAVE Except you can't can you. Men fuck. Women get fucked. Goodbye.

THE BAND

NEW TOWN HUMANS are waiting for ADAM.

ADAM enters.

ADAM Right then mother fuckers.

ROBBIE What?

ADAM I've got us a gig.

ROWAN You what?

ADAM Yep.

ALEX But we haven't got any songs.

ADAM Well we've got four songs, they're just not cohesive and that's not the problem.

MELANIE How is it not a problem that we're a band with a gig without any songs?

ADAM Because we only have to play one. This is our chance.

MELANIE How is it our chance?

ADAM Because this is the only place where all the people we want to talk to are definitely going to be.

ROBBIE Oh no.

ADAM Yes.

ROBBIE Oh for fuck's sake we can't do it at the—

ADAM That's right we're doing it at the prom.

ROWAN You fucking what.

MELANIE Everyone is going to be there.

ADAM Exactly.

ROBBIE When is it?

ADAM Next week.

ALEX We've got a week to write and learn a song?

ADAM Yeah. Easy.

ALEX How easy.

ADAM Well you haven't played us your song yet.

ROBBIE I've got mine.

ADAM Really?

ROBBIE Yeah. It's about horses.

ADAM Right. So just to be clear. You've written a song about… Horses

ROBBIE Yes.

ADAM You know the whole point of NEW TOWN HUMANS is a sort of anti-bullying/macho bullshit thing don't you.

ROBBIE I do yes.

ADAM So how have horses got anything to do with that

ROBBIE Well I'll fucking show you if you shut up won't I! Slight disclaimer, I didn't know we were gonna do it at prom.

You Neigh
The price of my love's not a price that makes you want to stay
You Trot
In your fields which you shit in the middle when you see me pop by
Why so sad?
Remember what you promised me when I brought you here
Now you're making me mad
Remember, how you feel about me, I'm the one.

You'll love me, soon you'll see
You'll see that you're in love with me
You'll love me,
Time will tell
When I tell you how I feel you'll swell
Horses run,
Riders fall!
We will see each other through it all
And when trot turns to run
I will tell you all my dreams of you to remind you of my love

You say I ride you too much and you can't go on
You'll be the one complaining when I am gone...
And no, don't say you don't know!
'Cause John I know you know!
John I fucking love you
John you I know I love you
I have done and will do Forever
and ever and ever and ever and ever...

You'll love me,

John you'll see
You'll see that you're in love with me
You'll love me,
Time will tell
When I tell you how I feel you'll swell
Horses run,
Riders fall!
We will see each other through it all
And when trot turns to run
I will tell you all my dreams of you to remind you of my love

ROWAN Genuinely thought that was great.

ADAM Yeah we're nearly there.

ROBBIE Well what was wrong with it?

ADAM We'll it's a bit… specific. Like we all know Robbie's gay, well we don't know who John is, that's a question for another time, but it's not like… This isn't all our concern, it's his concern. It's the feminism thing all over again. Robbie it's boss you're gay and you're confident. If you sing that at prom, it's not going to go well (we're not that revolutionary). We need to speed things up. Alex have you got yours?

ALEX It's nearly ready. Tomorrow. I promise tomorrow.

DAVE

DAVE I don't see the point in this.

TIM This what?

DAVE This cycle, this go to the pub, this get pissed, this hope for something to happen, this constant round and round and round and round and round of endless fucking nothing. This town is a fucking void and I'm just falling into it.

TIM Alright mate no need to get deep.

DAVE I'm not getting deep mate it's just what's the point. We're not going anywhere. We're all the same. We're literally all exact fucking clones.

TIM Shut up.

DAVE Don't tell me to shut up.

TIM I dunno why you can't just enjoy yourself.

DAVE Because there's nothing to enjoy. We're just getting older pretending to be kids. Some of us are getting married. And none of us are doing anything other than what's expected.

TIM Why would we?

DAVE What?

TIM Why would we do anything other than what's expected?

DAVE Because that's life. That's what we should be doing. We should be choosing to have adventures. To live.

TIM What about staying still? Planting roots in a community. Being who you were supposed to be. Making this place amazing? Serving the fucking place that made you. What about that? You owe this place, it's disrespectful to think about leaving.

DAVE Maybe.

TIM Have a drink. We'll watch the footy. Then we'll go out. And it'll be boss.

DAVE You're not listening. We're just drinking and getting fucked to escape that we're not doing anything. That there's nothing to look forward to. That this place isn't enough.

TIM It is. There's everything here. There's houses. Nature. Cinemas. Women. Everything. What more do you want?

DAVE I dunno. I would have liked to have been something different.

TIM Stop being gay. Drink.

DAVE Yeah. Maybe you're right.

THE PLAY

DEAN Can I be honest?

JAMES Yeah.

DEAN I thought it was shite.

KIRSTY Why?

DEAN Because it was exactly how I said it was going to be.

JAMES The reviews are gonna be great. Just. Chill.

DEAN Yeah because you've got arts reviewers from the city coming.

JANET They know what they're talking about.

DEAN Exactly. And that's the last thing you want from a critic. You want someone who doesn't know what they're talking about. You want people who just happen to be there looking for something to do. Someone like the audience. That's how you can tell if it's good or not. And they looked bored.

JAMES That's not how it works. Critics like it. People change their mind and suddenly everyone loves it. The same people that were bored will be tweeting that we're the next Complicité.

DEAN the wa?

JAMES Just a theatre company. It's a London thing

DEAN You see all that's the fucking problem. The whole problem is that you've got someone, and please don't be offended by this, you've got someone who hasn't lived here for years, has been living in a city where people will pay any price to do anything that sounds quirky, coming here, showing some mad irrelevant culture to people who live here, telling them what they think is good for them and then being judged by some other wanky cunt who doesn't live here telling him he's doing a great job when everyone else is just lost.

JANET It wasn't that bad.

DEAN This is the problem. We're kidding ourselves that we thought it was good when we're doing the same stuff that causes all the shit in the first place.

KIRSTY You're being emotional because you were proved wrong.

DEAN No I wasn't proved wrong. No. Listen right. Yeah. I said you have to talk to people who live here to work out what's right, right? I said that. And you didn't do that. And what's happened is that you've read in *The Guardian* about masculinity and you've been to a few fancy shows and you've just applied both those things to a play and you've made a thing that means every young man who needed to hear all that has been put off because they thought it was wanky and patronising. That's what's happened. You've made them not listen. And you've made them not want to come back. They won't. Now I don't want to say that your intentions are wrong, they're not, they've just come from the wrong place and then you've done them badly. That's it.

KIRSTY I thought it was great.

DEAN Well you fucking would Kirsty because you're posh.

JAMES Alright no need for that.

DEAN I'm sorry I'm sounding like a dick.

JAMES No maybe you're right.

DEAN I'm just saying if you want to serve a community you've got to fucking talk to it. And listen to it. Engage with its concerns because that's how we fucking ended up with this soulless place anyway. I love it but look it's just houses and a shopping complex because that's all that they think they need to provide and we know it. We all know it. We know we're on a mad cycle of drinking and eating and working and watching populist TV and yeah that's probably exactly why we need a theatre right, yeah of course, but this town is a direct result of politicians doing what we've just done now. They've gone 'we need to make something, let's do houses, shopping complex, pubs, done'. When we do it next time–

JAMES What?

DEAN This is a good idea James I just think you're a helmet.

JANET Why don't you write it next time?

JAMES What?

DEAN Yeah what?

JANET You know this town don't you. You know what people like actually want to do. Why don't you write it?

DEAN I can't write.

JANET Of course you can. You chat all the time. Literally all the time. You've got a lot to say you've just gotta make it a story and make it something your mates would actually do and actually care about... make a good night for your mates, and ya mum, and family. It's not hard. What we made was hard because it was ridiculous and pretentious but you know what's actually good. Why not? We'll spend ages talking to people about what they want to do and what to see and how they want to see it and where they want to see it. that's gotta be better than that.

JAMES Janet.

JANET He's right they were bored shitless.

DEAN You think I could write it?

JANET Well I do yeah

JAMES I dunno –

JANET If we're being honest James right now this is like... I dunno. A bit shit. Isn't it. What have you got to lose?

JAMES My company.

JANET If you carry on making work like this you've lost it anyway. I think he should write the next one.

DEAN I can't write.

JANET Well then, we should make it together. Asking that question all the time whether it's worth doing here, now, in this way. You're talking sense. I'd rather make work that people like, than people think is wanky.

KIRSTY I might be busy.

JANET Whatever I don't care. But I'm just saying that's what I want this to be, because you're right you just need someone like me to help you. You need to listen to the town and to us. Maybe Dean doesn't write it but we do it together.

JAMES You're right

DEAN OK? Now let's jib this and get a pint.

KIRSTY Slug and Lettuce?

JAMES Just fuck off Kirsty.

THE BAND

ADAM Right then.

ALEX This all feels a bit personal

ADAM That's exactly what it should be.

ALEX Is it supposed to be this raw?

ADAM Yes.

ALEX Why?

ROBBIE Because that's art isn't it. Like being fucking…
Human.

ALEX OK.

> *I am scared*
> *Scared of Love*
> *Scared of love and lust.*
> *I was 14*
> *He came to me*
> *He told me he loved me*
> *And he kissed me in the rain.*
>
> *We fell in love*
> *He met my parents*
> *He came round for me*
> *And I let him and he made me*
> *Video me*
> *Do things and he told me he loved me*

I hear him laugh
Fingers at me
Fingers at me
Drooling mouths and laughter

To him I was a conquest
Something to be won
To prove his status
As a chosen one.

I am a victim
A casualty of war
No longer a human
But someone who is done.

ROWAN That was beautiful.

ADAM No. I think we have to find a way to tell all of these stories and all of these sounds in one big… thing. I've got an idea.

KATIE

KATIE We're in Nando's. I've chosen Nando's because I know he likes it and around us is that smell that makes everyone feel at home. That chicken smell. He's been coming to this Nando's with his family since he was like eight so I've brought him here and I'm going to ask him out right because if I don't ask him I'm going to go mad. He's wearing his Fred Perry T-shirt, the one he wears for special occasions. He looks nice and I'm looking at him, I'm looking at him right here and I can just see something in his eye and I can't tell you what it is I can't like put my finger on it but it's something and there's something that's not quite there. It's like a part of him is missing and I can't

77

tell you I can't...I can't say what it is it's not a deadness
it's just a... It's just a sort of... He's just not quite there and
he's smiling and he's laughing but when he looks down
at his chicken it's like he's alone and he's himself and
that's why we're here. That's why we're in Nando's eating
Lemon and Herb half-chickens because I need to ask
him... I need to ask him what's up and I need him to talk
because if he doesn't talk then there can never be... We
can never have...

Are you OK?

And he looks at me and he smiles. And says

Yeah. I'm fine.

It's OK to talk you know.

And he says 'I'm fine'.

You can talk to me.

And he says 'Why are you being weird?' and in myself
I'm like welling up because I'm not the one being weird.
I'm the one looking out for him. I'm the one looking out
for us. I'm the one that's trying to be you know... Trying
to be like a fucking partner here.

I'm telling you there's something wrong with you and I
want you to talk to me.

And he's quiet now. I think that he's about to say
everything I want him to that he's sad and he wants help
and I want to say let's talk about it, let's go and get a
drink and sit in a pub and drink red wine and listen Otis
Redding and talk and talk and talk and just get it out and
talk and talk and talk and maybe I can talk about me and
we can finally have a relationship that's like I have with
my mates and we can stop playing at being boyfriend and

girlfriend and actually like... Be there for each other. And he looks at me. And he goes –

You're a fucking pyscho.

And I don't know what to say to that. Every vein in my body is imploding because I know – I know that if I kick off like I wanna kick off then I'm confirming everything he's saying is true. I am a pyscho. But I'm not. All I want. All I want is to be able to talk to my boyfriend. All I want is to be able to have a relationship where he can say how he feels and stop being so fucking sad and I can do the same. I sit there. And I say: I need you to talk to me. And he says...

I don't want to do this anymore.

And he goes. A part of me wants to stop him. A part of me wants to grab onto him and tell him that we can work through this. A part of me wants to say as a friend you need to talk. But I don't. I let him go. And I sit there. In Nando's. With the half-eaten chicken. Wondering how I'm going to get home. And wondering if it's just him or if I'm going to have to spend the rest of my life falling in love with sad men, getting their sad all over me, and wondering if I'll ever love a man as much as I love my friends.

LARDER

A boy walks on with some rope.

LARDER Hello.

JIM Hello.

LARDER What are you doing?

JIM I'm just... Nothing really.

79

LARDER What's that?

JIM Just some rope.

LARDER You making a swing?

JIM Yeah. I'm making a swing. Going to go to the quarry and make a swing on the tallest tree I can find. And then swing on it.

LARDER Cool. Enjoy.

JIM Thanks.

He leaves.

JONNY & ROGER

ROGER Can I ask you something?

JONNY What?

ROGER Do you ever like –

JOHNNY What?

ROGER Do you ever feel like –

JOHNNY What?

ROGER Doesn't matter.

JOHNNY Georgina's put some pictures up on Insta of her in a thong.

ROGER Oh really?

JOHNNY Yeah.

ROGER Nice?

JOHNNY Yeah.

ROGER Cool.

JOHNNY Are you OK?

ROGER Yeah.

JOHNNY It's like you want to say something.

ROGER Na I'm cool. You're my best mate right?

JOHNNY Yeah.

ROGER Good.

JOHNNY Why you being gay?

ROGER Sorry yeah. Let's see Georgina's thong.

LARDER

I suppose it's time to be honest about why I'm doing this.
Why I'm trying to make sense of everything. Why I'm trying
to normalise everything.

OK. It's a summer's evening and I go for a walk. The air is
crisp. I'm walking through the hills and I can see the town
and the nature and the beauty and the everything and it's
quiet and suddenly, out of nowhere, literally out of nowhere
with no thought or provocation, it hits me. This weight. This
weight. And I don't know where it's come from. All I can
feel is this heaviness. This heaviness deep inside me. And
my mind is full of this darkness and I've realised it. And it's
consuming and it hurts, like physically hurts. My life now was
so full of distrust, meaninglessness, bitterness, lack of love.
And I walk right up to the Vue cinema. And I climb the fire
stairs. And it's slow. And it's heavy. And I'm right up there.

And I stand. And I imagine the world without me. I imagine the feeling of jumping off and feeling weightless and then feeling nothing. And then, just as I was about to jump, I look and I see someone else. I see this boy I've seen around for years. I see Dave.

DAVE

DAVE The world looks big from up here. Huge actually. You can see the whole town stretching out in front of you. Little grey houses and behind it just… nature spreading out for miles. From here it looks hopeful. Like – I dunno. Like something that's not just a hole sucking us all in. The sky is huge. Everything seems so big and I can feel… I can feel this tightness; this tightness wrapping itself around me this thing here, here in my chest and I… I don't want to die, I don't want to die I just want to not live and I can't explain it; I can't explain where it comes from or why it's here and it's all I can feel it's all I can think about it's all that is consuming me and I don't know where it comes from, I don't, I don't know where it comes from but it… but it… but it's here and standing here standing on top of the Vue cinema all I want to do is fall off the edge so that this might stop and people might see me and someone might bring me back to life and everything might be OK but it wont be, but it won't be, because that's not how life is… that's not, that's not… rainbows… that's not… cats… that's not… Mum… fuck Mum.

His phone rings.

LARDER

Seeing him I can see myself in pain. Suddenly I feel less
alone. I watch as he talks to his mum. I watch as he climbs
down to the path. I watch as he walks away. I go home. I
open Messenger. I ask him if he's OK. He says no. I say no.
We chat. Over the internet. We never do face to face. We're
just two people opening up through screens without having to
be scared of being vulnerable. We tell each other our stories.
I knew I could carry on because I knew it was normal. And
that's why I'm telling all this. Because all these experiences are
normal. We just have to talk about it to find a way through it.
We have to do something to make it easier. But I didn't know I
was going to do something until I saw a shit band at prom.

THE BAND

Glitter. Pheromones. Dancing.

The HOST sings.

THE HOST Thank you ladies and gentlemen. Welcome to
your prom. It's been a roller coaster of a few years but
you made it, congratulations. This is a difficult time in all
our lives and I want to thank you for being the wonderful
year-mates that I've grown to love. Ladies, I want to say
that I've never met such awesome powerful, kind, caring
supportive people in my life and I just know that you're
all going to go on and be the doctors, lawyers, architects,
actors, singers that you want to be. Boys, you know you've
been around and you've upset us a bit because most of
you are awful but there we are. From an RS perspective,
that's what I'm going to do at uni, I have one message.
Yes, God created Adam before Eve. But never forget; an
artist always makes a rough sketch before a masterpiece.
Now before we carry on this lovely heartfelt evening I've

been told to introduce the band NEW TOWN HUMANS who are going to play a song to their year to say goodbye.

NEW TOWN HUMANS come on in their rebellious costumes,. They play.

> *Do you ever feel like you're in the sea*
> *Drifting on away from home*
> *Wanting to come back in?*
>
> *Do you ever feel like you love this place?*
> *Like you know you can be happy*
> *But you know that you cannot be.*
> *Do you know that there's still a chance for you*
> *There is you in you*
> *Do you know that there's still a chance for you*
> *There is you in you*
> *You just gotta forget the fight*
> *And start to be*
> *Just own yourself*
> *Like Lady Gaga*
> *'Cause we are in heaven*
> *And you're burying yourself*
> *Tell them all to fuck off*
> *And let yourself fly!*
>
> *We are all pelicans*
> *Come on shake your tail feathers!*
> *Tell them to fuck right off*
> *Let yourself fly fly fly!*
> *You don't have to feel like a failure*
> *You're original, cannot be replaced*
> *If you only knew what the future holds*
> *Shake off the ideas that you hold in your place*
> *People you look up to are not happy*
> *Stop idolising them because it's making you sad*
> *Like a Pikachu, you'll be electric*

They all belong to something you don't need to be

You just gotta forget the fight
And start to be
Just own yourself
Like Lady Gaga
'Cause we are in heaven
And you're burying yourself
Tell them all to fuck off
And let yourself fly!

Baby you live in a perfect place
So show you real face
Stop trying to be him, her, them
History won't remember them

We are all pelicans
Come on shake your tail feathers!
Tell them to fuck right off
Let yourself fly fly fly!
You don't have to feel like a failure
You're original, cannot be replaced
If you only knew what the future holds
Shake off the ideas that you hold in your place
People you look up to are not happy
Stop idolising them because it's making you sad
Like a Pikachu, you'll be electric
They all belong to something you don't need to be

You're gonna start to be yourself
Fuck you, fuck you, fuck you
You're gonna start to be yourself
Fuck you, fuck you, fuck you
You're gonna start to be yourself
Fuck you, fuck you, fuck you
You're gonna start to be yourself
Fuck you, fuck you, fuck you

LARDER

LARDER No one laughs. There is awkward shuffling around on the floor and there are glances and people don't do much, they just stand and look at their shoes. It's broken only when someone shouts 'gay'. People laugh. The music starts and the night begins again. That's it. Everyone goes to back to their lives. Nothing changes.

And seeing them do that. Seeing them do something. Be brave. I knew that I have a responsibility to do something not just for me but for my home. Our town. It's full of men that are being forced to behave in a way that is unnatural. They're being told they have to behave like this when it's not them. They can live here and be themselves if they just let someone tell them that it's OK. Someone needs to tell people to stop being pervy little fucks. Tell people to stop trying to be seen as hard. Tell people to stop shitting on other people and tell them to be kind and empathetic. Then hopefully, maybe, someone else will feel better, and together you might not feel alone. This place has everything... It's fucking great. It has the potential to be everything. It's cheap and there's nature and if we all realise our role... We have to take responsibility for our community: which means calling each other out, which means making things happen, which means seeing what we need and acting on it. If we do that. Then maybe we can make this place fucking amazing. But to do that – we have to actually do something. And that starts with me. Doing this. And hoping you'll do something too.

Thank you.

The End.